# THE COACH'S

By Anna Marie Sinatra

# Table of Contents

## Forward:

Internationally recognized Coach, Consultant, Trainer & Speaker, Anna Marie Sinatra will partner with you in helping you to identify and zero in on where you're "Missing the Mark"; then tailor make a program specifically for you and/or your business/company to "Hit the Mark Every Time!".

## Introduction:

Whether I am presenting a workshop, a speaking engagement, or coaching an individual, I am often asked where I get my positive energy from. People are amazed at my ability in assisting them in looking at situations in their personal and business life in a new and more productive way. "How do you stay so positive, so energetic?", they ask, often followed by "What kind of training and/or degree do you have?" I am always quick to respond, "Are you really sure you want to know? Because I will tell you!"

This opens the door for me to share about how Jesus changed my life and how He continues to Bless me! Of course I refer them to my web site to check out my credentials and I offer them a peek at my portfolio. At the same time I remind them, that what they are seeing/feeling from me is the love the Father has for them, that is expressing itself through me. You see I take the Word of God seriously. When Jesus said don't just be hearers of the Word, but be doers of the Word as well, I believed He meant it!

What good will all the education around the Word be, if I didn't put it into practice in my daily life. Coming from years of self help books, workshops and seminars I have exhausted the many ways of searching for peace in my daily life. After coming full circle (a 40 + year journey), I am quite sure Jesus is the/my Master Teacher and my personal Life Coach. I tried to skip over Him time & time again, and I am sure glad that He never gave up on me! As I look back I can see that He had been equipping me over the years, to share with others, His Good News!!!

As you read this collection of articles written over a two year span, try to identify, not compare yourself to that person's story. Remember comparing is a pitfall. Look for where you can identify, relate your struggles and issues to theirs and watch for the tools/coaching techniques I used with each individual and with a bit of time and practice you too will find yourself "Hitting the Mark Every Time!"

**Author's Biography:**

*Anna Marie Sinatra is a Buffalo native who is committed to the growth and development of* **all** *individuals, organizations and corporations. She is committed to her community by empowering the people and businesses in Western New York. Coming from a family who have always been activists in this area, she learned at an early age to get involved, as to make a difference, not only in her community but in the individual lives of all those around her.*

*She began In the early 80's working with organizations such as The Massachusetts Community Center, The Butler Mitchell, Community Action Organization, Concerned Ecumenical Ministries etc., and Unity Church; in developing new programs of community interest and/or improve upon existing programs. She has utilized her skills in leadership development, diversity training, communication, organization, marketing and development with organizations such as Buffalo State College, Elim Christian Fellowship, Group Ministries, Unity Church, Langston Hughes, The Word Newspaper, Juneteenth of Buffalo and The National Conference for Community and Justice.*

*She also works with individuals coaching them in various areas to get into action and move through the area in which they are temporarily stuck; beginning a new business, relationships, sales slump, etc.. When needed she connects them with other people/organizations that might be helpful. She has been published locally as well as internationally. She is the host of the television program; Health Matters and co-host of the radio program; Changing the Atmosphere. She appears often as a guest speaker on several other Radio & TV Programs.*

*She holds many certificates of completion; Leadership Program for Women at Canisius College, Religious Studies at PTBI a division of Logus Bible College, Leadership and Communication skills by organizations/individual trainers such as Landmark Education, Dr. Roger Firestien-Creative Problem Solving, National Carrier Seminars, Re-Evaluation Counseling, diversity training and Toast Masters .*

*She served as a Board of Director Member; Immediate Past President of the Buffalo-Niagara Chapter of the International Coach Federation, Temple Community Development Corporation and The Sinatra Solutions Team.. She is a member of The International Association of Coaches and Coachville.*

4

*Anna Marie is the recipient of an International Coach Federation Award which reads in part, "Your ideas and the way in which you worked on the Committee attest to your personal and intellectual development, and the best qualities we wish for in a Coach." Presented at the International Coach Federation Conference, November 2005.*

*She has been commended for her achievement in the community by many public officials most recently including Mayor Byron Brown; Council members: Antoine Thompson(Newly elected State Senator 2007), David Franczyk, Dominic Bonifacio, Jr., Bonnie Russell, Brian Davis, Joseph Golombeck Jr., Michael Kearns, Michael LoCurto, and Richard Fontana; Legislators: George Holt and Demone Smith. Also she has been recognized by past officials: Legislator Lynn Marinelli, Assembly members Sam Hoyt and Carol Siwek, State Senator Anthony Masiello, Mayor James Griffin, Congressmen Henry Nowak, Commissioners David Echols and Thomas Griffin, Council members David Collins and Joel Giambra and Past President Bill Clinton.*

# Nancy's Story

Nancy wonders why she is the one next in line for that promotion but never gets it. She often feels like her fellow workers aren't loyal to her; that they often talk about her behind her back. She just isn't getting any joy from her job anymore and thinks maybe its time to look for another. Well, after just a couple of Coaching calls, its easy to see that Nancy herself is in the center of all the strife in the office.

She complains about her boss often to the others in the office and at the same time doesn't hesitate to report the remarks others make to the next person that she talks or should I say gossips with. The best part about this situation is that Nancy did not have any idea that what she was doing to others, the same thing that she hated that was being done to her! Sound familiar?

Until we interrupt our patterned behavior by taking a look at the whole situation, we can fool ourselves into believing we are a victim and/or at worst a martyr. When we take the time to talk/work out our issues with an objective outsider, we then have the opportunity to see ourselves reflected back. With a loving, nonjudgmental atmosphere we have the possibility to recreate ourselves. "Reframing", is what I like to call it. The behavior we want others to give us, is the behavior we must have first.

When Nancy began to take ownership of her actions, stop talking about her fellow superiors & workers, focus on the quality of her performance, the atmosphere around the office began to change. Over time, people watched Nancy's character develop. Her relationships began to change with those around her including her personal life as well! And after just a few short months, Nancy got the promotion she so desired!

*Although the Coaching situation is real, Nancy is the name used to protect confidentiality.*

## Lori's Story

Coach, Mentor, Personal Trainer; no matter what you call it – it works!!! Just as an athlete uses a Coach or Personal Trainer to prepare for victory, so must you!!! As a Coach/Consultant/Trainer I often hear stories of discouragement from those who have attempted wonderful goals and have fallen short of victory. I have heard it said, the cemetery if filled with good ideas. So what's the difference from one who has victory and one who just can't seem to make it happen?

These stories always include an array of reasons (I like to call it what it is – excuses), as to how and why they stopped reaching for their goals. I didn't feel well, there's no free time in my day, I don't have the skills, my husband/wife doesn't support me, I don't have enough money, the dog ate my home work, etc., etc.. You see the excuses, or do you still need to hear them as reasons, are what we use to justify not following through to victory. Feeling a little confused? Read on and try to see yourself in Lori's story.

Lori is a successful business woman working for a large corporation but always wanting to have her own business. She would often begin the steps in creating her dream but always got stopped by the idea that she didn't have enough time in the day to devote herself to take the necessary steps in creating her business. So during our coaching calls we would take a good look at where she was spending her free time. We looked at her mornings before she went to work; was she starting her day with God? His Word? Praying? Or was she hitting the snooze button a few times, then jumping out of bed in a whirlwind, rushing to get to work?

How about after work? How was she spending her time? Was TV a big part of her evening or could she utilize some of that time to begin the steps necessary to birth her new business. In most of my coaching situations when we're discussing beginning a new business, we utilize all free time to develop and begin manifesting the dream into reality. So if owning your own business is your dream, you must be ready to identify and give up you time wasters to create the time and space to manifest your dream!

Often times it's the small adjustments of the above mentioned, refocusing and staying on target with the help of a coach each week to assist you in realizing your victory. In Lori's case it went a little deeper. After a few coaching calls, Lori opened up and shared that she'd been having an affair with her supervisor. All those late working evenings, (excuses), where surely putting a strain on her time as she then saw it. As our coaching continued Lori began to open up about her true feelings about herself and her situation. Although she was attending a church sporadically, and obviously wasn't committed to living a life that reflected Jesus in her heart, she knew the truth and couldn't ignore it any longer! When she took the time to look, to cry, and to repent with an objective supporter, she knew she had to line herself up with God's Word. Ignoring the truth was not only stopping her in her business life, but was truly blocking her in all areas!

You see Lori was a single woman having an affair with a married man, insuring never to find a husband of her own! As we continued with our coaching calls, Lori began to see how committing herself to God first would then ensure success in all areas of her life. As she seeked Gods Will and Word for her life, her character began to develop and she also began facing her own demons that needed to be dealt with.

When we stop running from the truth and face it head on, we're then able to allow God to work from the inside out and make the permanent changes that will effect us in every area of our lives!!! Lori ended her dysfunctional relationship with the married man, committed herself to her Church and is utilizing Coaching to help her stay on target in all these areas including the dream of her very own business. I know success will follow her where ever she goes now!!!

*Although the Coaching situation is real, Lori is the name used to protect confidentiality.*

## Mary's Story

## New Year's resolution or change for life

So what's it going to be this year? Year after year the tradition rings in our ear – to resolute or not to resolute? That is the question!

Well if you're like most you vacillate for a while until forced into a decision because the d-day draws near. At times you've been filled with excitement and confidence that this year would be different. This year you'd take on the challenge and be victorious only to find that once again after a short time your resolution was a distant memory. Other times you realized that you never carried out your resolution anyway, so why bother in the first place! So now what? Read on and try to see yourself in Mary's story…

Mary has been trying for most her life to find contentment and happiness. She has searched in many ways in various places. Going from church to church, job to job, one relationship to another, one self help book and/or group to another, only to find that after years of struggling she really wasn't any further down the path then when she first started. How could this be she wondered. She worked so hard at trying to fix herself and everyone around her for that matter. It seemed so simple; learn/gather some information, cry a little, pray a little, force a solution she felt was best, and keep moving right along. BUT why wasn't it working? Why wasn't her life changing? Where was that peace hiding, that she so diligently searched for?

Having tried everything she could think of and most of what was suggested to her by her friends, she was open to some coaching in this area. I quickly pointed out to her that the common denominator throughout all her experiences was HERSELF! Confused by this we looked a little closer. In every relationship that didn't work what or who was the common denominator? In every job and church situation, who was the common denominator? HERSELF.

You see the problem was she took herself everywhere she went! She began to see that the problem wasn't out side of herself, it wasn't other people, other situations, it was herself! Feeling hopelessly defeated she turned to me and said so now what? I was excited to tell her the answer was simple. The answer was Gods Word! Learning Gods Word and applying it to her life was the answer. Sound familiar? Too simple to be true?! Go back and read it again!

Read that the answer is not just in learning BUT in applying as well. And this takes time! She committed to spend 30 minutes a day reading, meditating and praying. This began her process of changing her thinking, thus creating a world in which she tapped into the peace, contentment and joy she was searching for! Throughout our weekly coaching calls Mary always remembered to include time spent with God as part of her daily priorities!

You see there is a place deep down inside of us, that can not and will not be satisfied with anything short of the love and peace of God. Try if you must – fill it with drugs, alcohol, food, sex, work, exercise, TV, etc. BUT until you resolve in your own heart and mind that only God can fill this place, nothing in your life will truly change. This transformation will occur only from the inside out and is certain to change your life forever!  So consider the possibility of committing to studding and learning Gods Word to be the only New Year Resolution that you need!

Each day commit to finding just 30 minutes to read, meditate and pray on Gods word. Surely you can spare just 30 minutes a day to stop all the bouncing back and forth in your life that you have done! Surely you can spare just 30 minutes a day to find the peace you've been searching for, the peace that passes all understanding!

*Although the Coaching situation is real, Mary is the name used to protect confidentiality.*

# Rachael's Story

Coach, Mentor, Personal Trainer; no matter what you call it – it works!!! Just as an athlete uses a Coach or Personal Trainer to prepare for victory, so must you!!! As a Coach/Consultant/Trainer I often hear stories of disappointment from individuals who seem to get stopped in life and can't seem to figure out why. Whether it's in their personal, professional, or business life, the story's the same. They try and try to achieve a goal and/or behavior change, only to fall short of victory each and every time.

They get stuck in the same old, same old; feeling more depressed than the time before. The cycle seems to go on and on until a decision is made. Awareness is the first step in a behavior change, followed by a decision to take action, then creating a "Structure for Success", a blueprint if you will, that when followed, brings you to victory!

As you read Rachael's story, try to see yourself in her struggles and accomplishments:

Rachael has been beaten down by the seemingly atmosphere of defeat. During my first meeting with her, she talked about the many times she began the process of starting her own business. She would get real excited about the possibilities God placed before her, begin to take action in a defined direction, only to question her decision and motives, before she barely got off the ground.

I listened as she vented all the reasons why she wasn't good enough, all the reasons why the business couldn't possibly succeed and all the excuses, Oh I'm sorry – I mean the reasons why people wouldn't be interested in the product or service she was offering. It was no wonder why she couldn't move forward! As momentum would begin to form, the enemy whispered in her ear, all the negative points that eventually killed and destroyed her hope and enthusiasm.

Taking the time to jot down all those negative statements on a sheet of paper entitled F.E.A.R. = **F**alse **E**vidence **A**ppearing **R**eal, the process began as she began noticing when and how often these thoughts were attaching her! Seeing them on paper was extremely helpful. It got them out of her head and in a tangible form, so we could plan our counter attack!

Once this "noticing muscle" was developed, it became easier and easier for Rachael to notice the negative thoughts trying to penetrate her mind. After just a few coaching calls, she began to see the light at the end of the tunnel! Together we visited her decision making process, making sure God is ordaining her every step. This enabled her to move forward instead of going back and questioning. We replaced every negative thought with a positive statement. Because Rachael was a Christian, my job was easier! I just had to point her to Gods Word to find the truth about herself and her life.

Each week we talked, I reminded her of her of the awesome woman of God that she is, the commitment she made to this process, her commitment to Him, His Word, Prayer & Meditation, and her commitment to Gods people! She was encouraged and motivated to seek Gods Word for herself and is now moving forward in her business. As she looks back on all her trials, she notices that God was truly in every one of them. He had been equipping her all along. Her past experiences had given her a wealth of knowledge that she is now sharing with others, providing them with products and opportunities to make better health choices for themselves!

Questioning Gods Will for our lives is something we all go through from time to time. Taking the time to stop, ask and listen for Gods guidance will ensure our victory. We will be less likely to get stuck, if we do this first. If you haven't done it yet, it's never too late! If you're questioning yourself, stop everything right now and take the time to use the tools that are readily available to you!!!

If you always do what you always did, you'll always get what you always got! The time is now to try a new way. It's never too late to try Gods way!!! Just simply turn towards Him and ask for help. He will always answer your prayers!!!

*Although the Coaching situation is real, Rachael is the name used to protect confidentiality.*

# John's Story

Often times I am coaching clients who are not Christians. This provides me with the wonderful opportunity to use the "Principals" that I know work in my life with those who don't know Him yet! Whether I am presenting a workshop, a speaking engagement, or coaching an individual, I am often asked where I get my positive energy from. People are amazed at my ability in assisting them in looking at situations in their personal and business life in a new and more productive way. "How do you stay so positive, so energetic?", they ask, often followed by "What kind of training and/or degree do you have?" I am always quick to respond, "Are you really sure you want to know? Because I will tell you!".

This opens the door for me to share about how Jesus changed my life and how He continues to Bless me! Of course I refer them to my web site to check out my credentials and I offer them a peek at my portfolio. You see I take the Word of God seriously. When Jesus said don't just be hearers of the Word, but be doers of the Word as well, I believed He meant it! What good will all the education around the Word be, if I didn't put it into practice in my daily life.

What good would it be if I didn't carry the message to non-believers in a non threatening way? Others get to see the Word in action before they even know what hit them! I am quite sure Jesus is my/the Master Teacher and my personal Life Coach. There was a time when I tried to skip over Him, and I am sure glad that He never gave up on me! And now as I look back I can see that He has been equipping me over the years, to share with others who are in the same boat I was once in. I am honored and privileged to share His Good News!!!

John is a successful businessman. He manages an office of over 30 people. The company he works for is quite large and he is required to participate in by-weekly meetings, where the department heads report on their success and struggles. During our first meeting he was quick and proud to tell me how important his job is to him. How he strives to be the best supervisor/manager ever, wanting to prove himself because it is his first supervisory position. However he feels the need to develop himself professionally because although he feels quite confident in his everyday role with the individuals he supervises, he is very uneasy when he enters the board room and has to face his piers.

Fear overcomes him in this situation. Positive as his report may be, he can't seem to give it without stumbling over his words, sweating like crazy, and feeling like a complete jerk! He certainly is not communicating how well his department is doing. As soon as he's done he quickly resumes his position in his chair, arms crossed over his chest as he gazes down towards the floor occasionally looking up at the next person talking, which in every case, confirms in HIS MIND, how inadequate he really is.

Each week we Coached/talked we visited his many successes. My job, as I saw it was to have him "pause" and really feel the great feelings that came with his many successes. Taking the time to jot down these success on a "One Sheet" (piece of paper named "Successes"), assisted him to really notice and feel how well he was doing in one area. This opened the door for us to take a closer look at where he needed some assistance; what was going on in the Board room.

John began to open up and talk about how he felt he really didn't belong in that Board room, how everyone else had better/more education then he did how they had been with that company for a long time now and how uncomfortable he was wearing a suit! I pointed out how important it was to "look" the part of supervisor/manager.

I suggested he enroll the help of his wife in picking out a suit he could be comfortable in. This worked wonderful as she became his best cheerleader every time he'd put on his new suit! It helped boost his confidence level along with the occasional review of his "One Sheet" titled "Success"!
We began "noticing" his thinking process just days prior to the scheduled board meeting. As those negative thoughts tried to infiltrate his mind, he practiced "pausing", "taking a breath" and invited them to float back out as quickly as they floated in!

Being aware of our thought process takes some time practicing ways in which to interrupt that self defeating pattern. Just like working out in a gym strengthens our muscles, the more we practice "noticing" the stronger that muscle gets too!

I then suggested "Toast Masters", a wonderful tool in which to learn and practice public speaking. Having had experience with that organization I was able to offer John some tips on presenting powerfully. Along with the other work we were doing these tips/suggestions I made, seemed to be enough to catapult him to the next level of his Professional Development!

John is now confident, self assured and is a great asset to his company as a peer partner as well as a supervisor/manager of his department. He is so happy and content with the changes we made together, and he looks good too! It will be fun to watch and see where God will take him on his journey. For now I am grateful that I was able to plant some seeds!!!

*Although the Coaching situation is real, John is the name used to protect confidentiality.*

## Alyssa's Story

## Catapult Yourself/Your Business to the Next Level

As you read Alyssa's story, try to see yourself in her, as you identify your own issue and apply the same principals for the success you desire. No matter what is stopping you, you too can "Hit the Mark"! Once you gain awareness followed by a consistent effort of behavioral change, nothing can stop you - but you! Create your "Structure for Success" and begin to enjoy the fruits of your labor! Your "Structure for Success" will be as different as there are people on this planet.

Work with a Coach, Mentor, Spiritual Advisor, Peer Partner, someone who will hold you accountable to do what you say you'll do! Get the training you need and watch your confidence grow. And what a better time to start than right now! This is the time of Pentecost! There is help available to those who seek Him! It's His promise! So how about it? Why not "Resurrect" your New Years Resolution, (oh you thought I forgot?!), and recommitment yourself to the process that is guaranteed to work?!

When I first met Alyssa she appeared to be an introvert. She lacked self confidence but made it up in her knowledge, skills and training as an Interior Design Consultant. She had a gift for organizing and decorating office space as well as pulling together all the necessary elements to make your home extremely functional and beautiful. She wanted to create her own Interior Design business, but felt like she didn't know where to begin.

She had helped so many family and friends over the last couple of years, as she applied all her gifts and talents to each individual situation. Everyone that she worked with raved about their end results. But something was missing for her. She just couldn't seem to pull herself out of the "pit" she was in when it came to thinking about packaging herself in her very own business.

We took a look at her business card. White and plan, no pizzazz it was an outward expression of how she felt inside. The more we talked the more was revealed. I wasn't at all surprised to learn that her home office space was in complete disarray! It doubled for a storage room with boxes and junk all around! I heard once that we teach what we need to learn most. Well she was surely a perfect example! Our work together began with cleaning out the clutter in her mind and her office simultaneously.

We worked with her innermost thoughts, beginning to apply God's truth to her "mind" situation, and during the same time period she committed to spending 1 -3 hours a day, 3 times a week to cleaning, sorting, filing, and organizing her office space. She was so excited about the possibilities that began to open up almost immediately during this process! I too was amazed at her progress!

Together we redesigned her business cards, created a brochure and pricing structure. It didn't take long for the need to increase her prices as she became booked months in advance! God had been preparing her for such a time as this! She couldn't see it at first because she was stuck in seeing herself as she was in the past. Once she could wrap her mind around a vision of herself for the future – the future then became a distinct possibility!

Because Alyssa took a leap of faith, trusted in the process, stuck with it even when it felt uncomfortable she became one of my best success stories! Thank You Jesus!!! Thank you for your Word and your example. Thank you for living, dying and resurrecting possibilities for us!!!

*Although the Coaching situation is real, Alyssa is the name used to protect confidentiality.*

## Marty & Jean's Story Part I

## Hearing vs. Listening

I would like to thank those of you who have taken the time to e-mail and/or call me with your questions and/or comments. I really appreciate hearing from you. I am committed to you receiving value from these articles. So when you let me know the areas where you are struggling I can then write about others who are challenged in similar areas. Together we inspire and encourage each other as we reach for the mark, using the principals Christ came to teach us! Let us take on becoming doers of the Word and "Hit the Mark Every Time"!

Marty and Jean have been married for five years now. They have two children; a toddler and a new born. Life for them is filled with diapers, feedings, babies crying, lack of sleep and most importantly no free time, nor any time for just each other. With two small children to constantly take care of, Jean stays in a "mother" mode all the time. Now as good as this is for their children, it certainly doesn't work with her husband. Jean is constantly talking to her husband as if he is one of the kids!

She hovers over him making sure he is doing things the "right way" with each of the babies. Any time he strays from her way of doing things, she's right on top of him, correcting him, showing him the proper way of doing things. This goes on from the time he comes home from work to the time they all go to bed. Can you imagine week-ends?

Consequently Marty began burring himself in his work. This is where he receives his fulfillment. Feeling inadequate as a father, Marty strives more and more in his job, where he is appreciated and respected. His opinion not only matters, but is highly regarded as he overseas a large department from a very prestigious company.

This gives Jean yet one more complaint about her husband; he's always working, he's not committed to her and their children, he won't make time for them. Jean begins to make up a story in her mind, that he doesn't love her and their family; that they are not his priority. Can you see where this is heading? Because I had been coaching Marty in his professional development, I had first hand knowledge on how much he loved his wife and children and also how important his job is to him. So we were off to a great start. Jean was more than happy when he approached her to do relationship coaching.

All was needed was a safe place for each of them to be HEARD! They were committed to each other and to their family life which gave them the willingness to really listen to each other and to begin to hear then take small steps towards understand the other person's feelings and points of view.

Creating a safe, loving atmosphere was key here. Each of them had been accustomed to listening for the frustration in each others voices. The comments felt like put downs, so the reactions were defenssive. When we "paused" and revisited their commitments, it was easier for them to HEAR the complaint of their partner. I reminded them, "behind every complaint is a commitment". This is a fact.

Try it out for yourself. If someone close to you is complaining about something concerning you, it's because they are committed to something in that situation that is not manifesting itself. When we look behind the complaint where commitment was hiding, we then could then respond with love, creating an atmosphere for change. When we look from a higher prospective, Gods view, we can move past our fleshly reaction and respond with love.

I believe we are always coming from one, of either two positions; a call for love, or giving out love. The problem comes in how we go about doing it. So take a moment and "pause yourself"; take the time to self examine and see where you might be falling short of hitting the mark in some of your relationships. It's only then that you will be able to effect change; get the results you desire with some willingness to get/stay into action.

Marty and Jean were able to HEAR each other once again with just a little coaching. With each situation of concern they needed to talk about, we used these techniques along with some others to get the end result they both desired; a loving, close relationship. In time they will be able to practice these principals themselves during challenging times.

They reminded me, this was the way they were at the beginning of their relationship; always listening with a loving, nonjudgmental ear, ready to give support and encouragement. Somehow as time passes we begin to take each other for granted and our negative treatment of each other begins to slowly disintegrate our relationship. BUT it doesn't have to be that way. "Pause yourself"; take the time to examine YOUR behavior, mix it with Gods Word: husbands love your wives…. and wives respect your husbands…. Then you too can "Hit the Mark" in your relationship!!!

*Although the Coaching situation is real, Marty and Jean are the names used to protect confidentiality.*

# Marty & Jean's Story Part II

# Responding vs. Reacting

Remember Marty and Jean from last month's column? They have been married for five years, and have two children; a toddler and a new born. Life for them is totally filled up with caring for these two precious gifts from God. Last month we visited the idea of really *"hearing"* each other when discussing important matters, vs. just *"listening"* to the words spoken.

If you missed it, you might want to pick up last months issue and re-read it! It could possibly help you in some of your relationships. Whither is it a husband/wife, parent/child, supervisor/employee relationship; these tools can help! Try it! Take one small step today! Take one tool and apply it to your situation. Become not only a *hearer/reader* but also a *doer* and get ready to "Hit the Mark" in your relationships!!!

Whenever Jean would approach Marty about a complaint that she had with him, Marty would *"react"* by withdrawing. He would think and feel a barrage of negative emotions, which led him to retreat inward more and more. After years of this behavior it became his automatic *"reaction"*. Before Jean would even open her mouth, he was already in his *"reaction"* mode. This made effective communication near next to impossible.

Jean's *"reaction"* mode was her sarcastic mouth. Not being able to get her desired *"response"* from Marty, she would attack him with words. She was quick to let him know how and when he wasn't measuring up as a husband and father. She did this with insults and criticism. Neither Jean nor Marty were very happy. They seemed to have lost that love connection with each other that they both so strongly desired. How were they to get that back? Glad you asked!!!

With utilizing *"Coaching"* as a powerful tool, we were able to pause and take a good look at the situation. Tired from all the strife in their home, coupled with the two little angels God had entrusted them with, they had the willingness to take a good hard look at themselves. As I kept having them look beyond their complaints and identify the commitments they had to each other and their family, this opened up a new listening atmosphere. Marty could see that what Jean really wanted was a loving, committed husband who was emotionally and physically available to them.

Jean began to see that what she so deeply desired, she herself was creating the atmosphere for the opposite to happen. With determination and hard work from each of them, they were able to begin the process of *"pausing"* themselves when things weren't going their way. Taking a time out, refraining from outbursts, taking a deep breath, and re-focusing on their mutual vision/goals enabled them to *"respond"* to each other in an appropriate manner. It's not easy to change a behavior pattern, but with time and practice it got easier and easier! When Jean didn't feel as if Marty was being present with her and the kids instead of *"reacting"* with complaining, she *"responded"* by reminding him of how important he is to her and the kids and how much she/they needed and wanted him!

Marty was so moved by her new behavior change that he became motivated to change his behavior and found himself wanting to be with them more and more. Their time together became so precious to him, he couldn't wait to get home after working long days at the office. Because Jean softened her tone and reached out to Marty with kind/loving words she created the atmosphere for Marty to become more *"responsive"*.

Now it was Marty's turn to show an act of good faith by staying in action. Remembering not to get caught up in work and get home late, giving up some TV time to play with the kids, and offering his help with the many daily tasks of maintaining a home, was also key in this equation!

You see this is where the rubber meets the road. You who say you are so spiritual…. are you ready to show some fruits? Are you ready to feel uncomfortable as you kill off some of your fleshly desires and grow in your spiritual maturity and statue by applying a new behavior? A behavior that you choose *(respond),* rather than a you being run by your behavior *(reacting)*…I set before you life or death… so which do you choose?

   *Although the Coaching situation is real, Marty and Jean are the names used to protect confidentiality.*

# Matthew's Story

## Wherever you go...there you are!!!

Coach, Mentor, Personal Trainer; no matter what you call it – it works!!! Just as an athlete uses a Coach or Personal Trainer to prepare for victory, so must you!!! As a Coach/Consultant/Trainer I often hear stories of disappointment from individuals who seem to get stopped in life and can't seem to figure out why. Whether it's in their personal, professional, or business life, the story's the same.

They try and try to achieve a goal and/or behavior change, only to fall short of victory each and every time. They feel more depressed than the time before. The cycle seems to go on and on until a **decision** is made. **Awareness** is the first step in a behavior change, followed by a **decision** to take **action**, then **creating a "Structure for Success"**, a blueprint if you will, that when followed, brings you to victory!

Yes, so sorry to report, but it is true; where ever you go, you take you with you!!! Sound a little confusing? Well don't despair! As you read Matthew's story, try to see yourself in his struggles and accomplishments:

I found myself sharing a story with Matthew, I once heard a long time ago. The story was about a man who just couldn't find contentment with his life. So he decided it was his job that needed to be changed. So after months of searching he landed a wonderful new position with a bran new company. But that didn't seem to quite do it. The same feeling of discontentment began to surface once again. He then decided that if he was to leave his wife of several years, then he would be happy.

After all, he rationalized, they fought much of the time anyways, and rarely did they feel happy/content with each other. After months of a long, difficult divorce, he found himself single and unhappy once again! Well it must be the geographical cure that would do it this time! So the man decided to relocate to a different state, taking a new position within his company. For a few short months the man thought he finally arrived. He finally found happiness.

He felt contentment with his new position, in his new company, in a new (warmer) state, UNTIL the inevitable happened; he began a new relationship with a new woman and found the same old problems he had before. It took him all these years and all these changes to figure out that HE was the common denominator in each of these situations!

You see, where ever you go, you are there! No matter how hard you try, you can't get away from you! As Matthew and I discussed this reality on a deeper level, he began to see the possibility, that he himself was "finger pointing" at every thing outside of himself as the "problem", rather than looking inwards for the answer. Your outer life is a direct reflection of your inner thoughts. No Kidding! No hiding! No fooling! If you want to change your life, (in any area), you must begin on the inside.

Here lies the secret to lasting change. Go with in. Focus on yourself. Stop looking at others as the problem. Once we begin to practice this new way of being, we then can identify the issue, accept it as part of ourselves for the moment, then take appropriate action in making the inside changes necessary to bring forth that which we desire on the outside. And by the way, I have heard it called the God hole; the place within us that hungers for God.

That intimate relationship with THE Father, the one and only who can really fill us. Whether you have taken the relationship cure, the job cure, and/or the geographical cure, it's never too late to come home to the one place that will permanent fill that emptiness inside. I believe God put it there so that we always remember to seek Him first, on a daily basis. Just as we need air to breathe, food to eat, water to drink, He is the only thing that will fulfill that need each and every human being has! The need to love and be loved must begin with God, and His Word.

Begin with the Fathers love and watch all your relationships prosper! Begin with making one small decision that will further your spiritual development and watch your world begin to change. You can't fix everything all at once, but you can make one small commitment to do something different that will effect your present state of mind.

Try it. If you haven't committed to a Church – do so!

If you haven't committed to anything other than church on Sundays – commit to your Bible study! If you're not involved in any of your church groups – get involved! If you're not tithing your time – do it! Today make one small change. Take one step outside of your comfort zone and watch God work! I promise, when you knock, he will answer!!!

*Although the Coaching situation is real, Matthew is the name used to protect confidentiality.*

## Leah's Story

# ATTITUDE...is "10% what happens to me and 90% how I react to it."

The same principles that make a successful life make a successful business. Athletes use a Coach, and/or Personal Trainer to prepare for victory, to assist them in reaching their goals and so can you!!! As a Coach I partner with individuals and businesses to assist them in identifying their goals, providing them with a "mirror" if you will, enabling them to see themselves from another's perspective. With great appreciation one of my clients once called me her "human mirror"!

Together we identified and unlocked the things that have been blocking her, stopping her from achieving that which she most desired.

As you read Leah's story, try to see yourself in her struggles and accomplishments:

Leah came to me wondering why she found herself always feeling bad. There was a sadness that surrounded her. After years of counseling with a good therapist, she thought she was over her childhood experiences of sexual abuse done to her by her oldest brother. She felt she had been healed from this abuse because of all the work she had done in therapy and that she was now able to be in the same room with her brother without it affecting her in a negative way. Then why, she asked am I still feeling so low?

I noticed that in every coaching session, Leah was always apologizing. Every time I would point out something to her she would respond, "I'm sorry", in a very timid voice, much sounding like a small child. Even when I reflected this back to her she said, "I'm sorry"! As we continued with our coaching calls, and Leah stayed faithful to her homework, "noticing exercises", it wasn't long before she was able to begin to "interrupt" this patterned behavior.

Awareness of the words coming out of her mouth, her determination to overcome her feelings of sadness, her commitment to the process of coaching, began to change her ATTITUDE! You see she was still carrying around the same sad, victim attitude. Although she had done so much work to get to the other side, up until this point she hadn't seen that her attitude about the situation needed to be reframed in her speaking! Working on the emotional side with counseling on the past issue, now enabled her now to become coachable, so we could address her present state of mind focusing on the future.

We took time to list the many things she was grateful for. We worked with the process of forgiving herself and her brother, gaining understanding for her abuser. We worked hard at Leah beginning to take re-spons-i-b-ality = her ability to respond to situations that she was truly responsible for, vs. feeling of inadequacy causing her to apologize for her very existence! Leah began to "love the rose for its beauty, instead of hating it for its thorns", "see the cup half full instead of half empty", etc.. Many clichés, but non the less still very meaning full.

So you choose. Choose something different this time. Challenge your thoughts. Begin by saying to yourself, "There must be a better way of looking at this". Or if that's too much of a stretch for you try, "There must be ANOTHER way of looking at this".

Ask God for help and ask Him to help you see the help when He sends it! Don't let yourself be so bogged down with your situation/challenge that you don't even see the help He sends. There is a way though! It's all in his Word, AND we all need help from time to time to understand, hear, to see ourselves/our problems/challenges from a higher prospective; Gods prospective.

What you focus on expands! So focus on His Word and then DO what HE says to DO: *"Finally, beloved, whatever is true, whatever is honorable, whatever is just, whatever is pure, whatever is pleasing, whatever is commendable, if there is any excellence and if there is anything worthy of praise, think about these things." Philippians 4:8*

Enjoy a favorite quote of mine by Charles Swindoll. Cut it out! Hang it on your mirror along with the above scripture and read it everyday for at least a month and watch your attitude begin to change!!! *"The longer I live the more I realize the impact of attitude on life. Attitude, to me is more important than facts. It is more important than past, than education, than money, than circumstances, than failures, than successes, than what other people say or do. It is more important than appearances, giftedness or skill. It will make or break a company, a church, a home. The remarkable thing is we have a choice everyday regarding the attitude we will embrace for that day. We cannot change our past. We cannot change the face that people will act in a certain way. We cannot change the inevitable. The only thing we can do is play on the one string we have, and that is our attitude. I am convinced that life is 10% what happens to me and 90% how I react to it. And so it is with you...We're in charge of our attitudes."*

*\*Although the Coaching situation is real, the name has been changed to protect confidentiality.*

# Mark's Story – Part I

## Create success wherever you go

Whether I am presenting a workshop, a speaking engagement, or coaching an individual, I am often asked where I get my positive energy from. People are amazed at my ability in assisting them in looking at situations in their personal and business life in a new and more productive way. "How do you stay so positive, so energetic?", they ask, often followed by "What kind of training and/or degree do you have?" I am always quick to respond, "Are you really sure you want to know? Because I will tell you!". This opens the door for me to share about how Jesus changed my life and how He continues to Bless me!

Of course I refer them to my web site to check out my credentials and I offer them a peek at my portfolio. At the same time I remind them, that what they are seeing/feeling from me, is the love the Father has for them, that is expressing itself through me. You see I take the Word of God seriously. When Jesus said don't just be hearers of the Word, but be doers of the Word as well, I believed He meant it! What good will all the education around the Word be, if I didn't put it into practice in my daily life?

I am quite sure Jesus is the/my Master Teacher and my personal Life Coach and that the Bible is my blueprint for living my life! As I look back I can see that He has been equipping me over the years, to share with others, His Good News!!!

Want to be successful in all your endeavors? Want people to light up when you enter a room? Want your husband and/or children to appreciate you? It's quite simple, get out of yourself and into them! What do I mean? Glad you asked! Let's take a look at Mark's story:

Mark has been in business for about one year now. He had a wonderful idea that could have sky rocked from the onset! One big mistake – he never developed the concept of "customer service". Oh yes, we've heard that term over and over again – BUT let's take a closer look. Mark was full of ......himself! He believed he knew what was best in every situation regarding his business. He never took the time to ask others what they wanted, how they felt, how they would like to see his store look, what they valued and what would keep them coming back for more.

Even in our short term Coaching Calls, I found him to be challenged whenever I offered a different perspective from his own. He'd listen reluctantly and still do things his own way. Of course as the owner of his business I was clear he always had the final say in making decisions, but he couldn't get out of himself long enough to find value in another's ideas, even his Coach whom he was paying to do such! Needless to say our coaching agreement lasted only a couple of months. He was very verbal about appreciating my services much to my surprise!

Today Mark is out of business. He's still doing what he loves but not the way he envisioned it. It was his hearts desire to have his own business that would grow and develop over the years. Had he been more "coachable", more open to ideas and input, his vision might have manifested. You see if you want to succeed in anything in life, whether it is your business, professional or personal life you must come from the prospective of serving others. Not like a slave of course but coming from a place of genuine love and wanted to serve a need in another.

If you truly care/love/believe in your particular product and/or service you've got half the battle won! The second part of this is to meet people where their at! This is what Jesus did. He won people over because he truly loved them AND met them where they were at! He didn't force feed, judge or criticize them. He respected their right to choose inside of offering them a better way. So hears the plan– examine yourself, your motives, and your heart. Are you in it just for the money, the power and/or the prestige? Or do you truly desire to add to and/or make a difference in other's lives?

Are you asking questions about them and really listening to their answers or are you too busy telling them all about you/your product? Will your product and/or service meet the persons need or are you just trying to close the deal? Always remember two things: Where you're coming from MATTERS and what holds true in business is true in our personal relationships. Take the time today to self examine and begin creating success everywhere you go!

*Although the Coaching situation is real, the name has been changed to protect confidentiality.*

# Beth's Story – Part II

## Create Success Every Where You Go

Want to be successful in all your relationships? Want people to light up when you enter a room? Want your husband, children and friends to appreciate you? It's quite simple, get out of yourself and into them! What do I mean? Glad you asked! Let's take a look at Beth's story:

Beth came to me several years ago. She was having a difficult time facing life on life's terms. She got upset when things didn't go her way. Her husband was impossible, her children were ungrateful, as well as the people she worked for! She was often frustrated feeling like she was going no where fast. "Why", she would ask? Why can't they understand me? Why can't they see things differently? Can't they see I am trying so hard?

It was clear to me that we needed to get to the core belief system that was running her. Asking several questions such as "What is most important to you?", "If I had a magic wand, and there was nothing stopping you, what would you being doing right now?", and most importantly, "Who are you really and what do you believe is your purpose in life?" It took a few coaching calls and lots of introspective homework on her end. Because she was a Christian we were able to pray together before and after each call which got her in the practice of praying and asking for God's guidance every time she sat down for her quiet time with pad and pen in hand!

She was so tired of trying to do things her way; she was ready for God to move in her life! She even began taking her Bible into her quiet time! She became more and more coachable as she began to get understanding. She began to see that she needed to give the exact same thing that she was seeking from others! Interrupting the pattern of "nobody understands me" gave her access into seeing that others around her felt the same way!

This is a high form of spiritual maturity; to see others as God sees them. Not to react to their dysfunctional behavior but to see that everyone is really doing the best they could in every given situation. Even though it might not look it, even though it might not feel it, we give up the need to be right and see them through a different lens. One particular lens that really works for me and most of my clients is remembering that in any given moment everyone is either one of two things; extending Love or calling for Love. Got it? Read it again, ponder it and remember to ask God for understanding! He'll show you!!!

Now I realize that some of this might sound very simplistic and in some ways it is. The most important part I can offer you is to begin somewhere! Begin noticing how you are thinking, talking. Begin to interrupt your thoughts, thank them for sharing, and invite them to leave! Try saying, "up until now I felt this way, but today I choose differently"; fill in the positive statement to fit your situation. You'll be amazed how powerful these tools are!

It didn't take long for Beth to begin to see the changes in her life. When she gave up the right/need to be right, listened to others from her new lens, she saw things quite differently! She was able to meet others at their need thus meeting her need as well! New behavior takes lots of practice. Working with me as her

Life Coach, I was able to work/train with her intensely and hold her accountable each week for the desired changes/commitments she made during each coaching call.

You too can create success everywhere you go. Changes begin with one small step AND keep stepping! Don't stop short of the miracle! Keep pressing towards the mark! Don't give up on your dreams/desires and they won't give up on you. Take responsibility for your life, stop blaming others for what doesn't work and watch your life catapult to the next level!

*Although the Coaching situation is real, the name has been changed to protect confidentiality.

## Anna Marie's Story

## Connect With The Higher Source

So often I am asked how I am able to stay so positive and focused. Always my response stays the same; my answer is in Gods Word. I live, breathe and eat the Word of God. Never before would I have guessed that my home today would contain several different translations of the Holy Bible. Never before would anyone who knew me bet on me graduating from Bible College. And never in my life would I ever imagine that I would be in Church on Sundays for up to five hours!

I am so grateful that God led me to a man that would help me to understand and embrace Jesus' teachings. A man that would point me right to the Alter of God, encourage me to keep pressing on, and give me a hunger for Gods presence that kept me coming back. That man is Pastor T. Anthony Bronner, Elim Christian Fellowship, my Pastor, my Church home/family.

When I look back over my life I can see that God has been equipping me all along! Everything I've gone through, every situation, every person, He's put in my path, has been to grow and develop me into the woman I am today. In gratitude and thanksgiving I offer myself back as His faithful and trusted servant, carrying the good news in my heart, sharing it with anyone I come in contact with, by being that Love. Accepting/meeting people where their at, is the only way to show them the Father!

So as you can see this month I choose to write about myself instead of one of my clients. My goal is to encourage you during this amazing season of the ultimate gift - LOVE. To encourage you as this New Year begins; to look at your life through a new lens, feel the Fathers Love; then express that Love everywhere you go! Looking back at my example, we can see that even through the most difficult times, the darkest days, God was always present.

As we grow and mature in the Word we KNOW that everything happens for our highest good. As mature Christians we NOW go through with a confidence in turning towards the One who will walk with us on our journey. The one who will help us get through to the other side with a new understanding, knowing and confidence. And this, my brothers and sisters will strengthen our "going through" muscles for the next time, for we surely know life is filled with a next time!

Now let us not forget the whole purpose of this journey is to help each other! God hasn't brought you through just for you. It's now your turn to show your gratitude and thanksgiving by standing with someone in need. Give the best gift you can this New Year: LOVE. Give of yourself. Write someone a note and tell them how much they mean to you. Go make amends to someone you've hurt. Offer your service to an organization that is in the business of helping others. Be LOVE. Give LOVE. Express LOVE - all for the one who gave His ultimate sacrifice of LOVE.

So while the gates of LOVE are wide open following this Christmas season – hop into the New Year with Love! Get creative in how you will express that LOVE. Remember if you want more love in your life, you've got to give more love!!! Love isn't love till you give it away. Be the love you desire and watch it flow back to you; pressed down, shaken together and running over!!!

## Peter's Story Part I

## F.E.A.R.
## False Evidence Appearing Real

I have heard it said that the grave yard is filled with good ideas. Well I'd like to expound on that: all my clients have wonderful ideas, some of which began to take action and then stop, others continue to dream about "what could be if only". Few are diligent enough to follow through to completion, reaping the rewards of sacrifice and hard work.

The excuses are many; life always gets in the way of what "we'd rather be doing", how "we rather be living", how "we wish we had our dream job/business. Today it is my prayer that you'll see yourself inside of Peter's story and begin to make small changes that will assist you continuing on the road to success, however that looks for you.

Peter loved to be outside. No matter what the weather, he was happiest when he could be outside gardening, tearing down or creating structures, working on cars, just about anything as long as it was outside. Peter was gifted and talented in working with his hands. He had acquired many skills over his life time that was of great value to those of us who are not gifted in the same! He frequently complained about his job as a maintenance man for a mid size company. He really didn't want to work for someone else; instead he was always entertaining the dream of owning his own business.

He worked many nights and week ends doing odd jobs for those who knew of his talents. So good, he often had to turn referrals away. So when he came to me for Life Coaching, it didn't take long for me to locate the source of his lack of enthusiasm for life, was coming from his disappointment of self; allowing himself to be blocked/stopped because of F.E.A.R. (False Evidence Appearing Real).

We worked with a "F.E.A.R. One Sheet". This is where you list the fear acronym listed above, at the top of a piece of paper (or a journal if you use one), and begin to "notice" your thinking, jotting down the negative thoughts that float in. Sounds like a very simple exercise and it is! But extremely powerful!!! You see you can either allow your thoughts to run you OR you can take control and run your thoughts! As you work this new muscle, "noticing", you begin to have access to awareness.

It's as though you put on a new pair of glasses and begin to see clearly; your thoughts are making you behave in ways you'd prefer not to. As Peter worked with this exercise, noticing his thoughts and jotting them down, they began to have less and less power over him. With each negative thought we created a new TRUTH statement. Peter began to work with those statements as he would visualize the negative floating out (as easy/quickly as it came in) and replaced it with the Truth of the situation.

His noticing muscle became stronger and stronger week after week until he/we felt he was ready to begin to take the steps in creating his very own business! Peter was now moving past that which once stopped him!!! He was ready to name his business, make his first business card, list his professional services on a flyer and brochure and begin to market himself. As he was already a man of integrity and excellence it didn't take long before he had enough clients to sustain him, that he could leave the security of his day job and work full time for himself!

Of course there was a lot more Coaching that went on then what could be listed here, but the point is; YOU can do what your heart is calling you to do, if you're willing to step out of your comfort zone and REALLY go after your dream.

So how about it? What's the New Years Resolution you made? Are you still on the road to success? Or have you given up on your dream, your self? Consider the possibility that there are underlying thoughts that you're not even aware of, that are running your life. Try this exercise. You've got nothing to loose but your old negative results! If you keep doing what you've always done, you'll always get what you always got! Try something new and let me know how it works for you! Next month I'll give you more tools that will assist you in "Hitting your Mark Every Time"!

*Although the Coaching situation is real, the name has been changed to protect confidentiality.*

The Coach's Playbook For Life~

## Peter's Story Part II

## There must be another way of looking at this

Thank you to all of you who gave me tremendous feed back on last months article about Peter. I am so happy to know that this column is a blessing to so many of you. It is my honor to be allowed to share with you, tools that will make a difference in your life as you begin to apply them to your everyday situations! I am continually energized as you share with me your success stories with me! Keep them coming! To God be the Glory!!!

As you recall Peter began working with a "F.E.A.R. One Sheet", (False Evidence Appearing Real); jotting down all those negative thoughts that permeated his mind as he began the exercise of "Noticing". Being passionate about creating change in his life, Peter was diligent in this process. He was amazed at all the negative thoughts that were constantly floating in, and equally amazed at how he could change things around by simply staying aware of what was going on in the back of his mind. I like to call this our back ground conversations.

Instead of our thoughts running us, we can and will take control of our thought process by utilizing a few simple steps, thus living our lives on purpose with intention. Peter moved along quickly in this process because he was a Christian, knew the Word of God, the Truth of the situation, and was willing to do what it took to effect change.

As we continued to work together week after week, Peter now had access into moving past his "blocks". We took each negative thought written on his "F.E.A.R. One Sheet", and interrupted this pattern using the statement, "up until now". Three little words that will change your life! And this is how is sounds, "Up until now I believed I wasn't smart enough, good enough, educated enough (fill it in for yourself), but now I see the Truth. I believe I am capable, I am enough, I can do this (again fill it in for yourself).

Up until now, interrupts, stops the thought from continuing on and opens up a clean clear slate on with to build upon! Working together with a Coach can assist you in catching these patterns on a regular basis. You would be surprised to see how, when, where and why these negative thoughts creep in! A good Coach will point out your speaking patterns, as it is a direct line to your thinking process. Catch this and change your life forever!!!

*Although the Coaching situation is real, the name has been changed to protect confidentiality.*

# Peter's Story – Part III

## There Must be Another Way of Looking at This

Your tremendous feed back has indicated the great need we all have as we face each day in our human existence, struggling with the blocks that keep us from realizing our true potential. This month we will continue to look at Peter, as he is moving past his blocks utilizing the tools of Coaching; "Noticing Exercises" then writing on his "F.E.A.R One Sheet", (False Evidence Appearing Real), and then moving into the next faze, "There must be another way of looking at this". Now if you're a bit confused, you'll have to pick up past issues of The Word, to "boot up" your knowledge of these tools, as we have discussed them in length in previous issues.

Today we are taking a deeper look at creating a future based on unlimited possibility rather than our automatic unconscious thinking process, that comes form our past experiences (in most cases our negative past experiences).

If you always do what you always did you'll always get what you always got. Intentional living/thinking requires effort. Our unconscious background conversation in our mind is always going on regardless if we're aware of it or not. So beginning to notice when, what and how we're thinking, compiled with writing about it begins to diminish its power over us. It no longer has a strong hold on us because we are exposing it to the light. As we continue to do this we grow that muscle, gaining strength in that particular area. We're then ready to create our future filled with unlimited possibility.

In Peter's case these three steps were invaluable to him! He began with Business Development Coaching, creating success in and around his business by getting out of his own self, his own way of thinking; into developing the skill of being able to see situations from others perspective. Always remembering, "there must be another way of looking at this", caused him to intentionally search for and in many cases really *hear* the other persons concerns/ideas.

People wanted to do business with him because they felt as if he really listened to them, that he really cared about them, and they were right!!! This created a wonderful atmosphere in growing his business. It didn't take long for him to notice that it was trickling down into his personal life as well. His wife, family and friends noticed the difference in him and they too moved into the atmosphere of corporation and consideration.

Now there are those exceptions; those people/situations that just won't respond to your new way of being but remember even Jesus couldn't reach every single person/situation. So do your best, keep your conscious clean, shake the dust off and keep stepping! Someone is waiting for a blessing so get going and affect your atmosphere!!!

*Although the Coaching situation is real, the name has been changed to protect confidentiality.*

# Patrick's Story

## Forcing Solutions = False Reality

Patrick had been running a successful business for nearly 10 years now and was enjoying the financial fruits of his labor. He had inherited the company from his Father who enjoyed success on a smaller level than Patrick was satisfied with. With much hard work and determination Patrick had taken that small family business and grew it in leaps and bounds nearly doubling its gross earnings to date.

One problem though, Patrick was micro managing every detail by working long hard hours not leaving any time for anything else in his life! And that's a whole other story! Where we began with our Coaching was looking at the employee turn over that was becoming a huge problem!

Patrick let go of a couple old employees he had inherited and a few left on their own. New people he brought in became weary after a few months working with him. No matter how competent they were, no matter how much training and instruction he gave them, he was unable to let them fly on their own. Every time they would attempt to step out within their scope of the business, making a decision and/or putting into action their way of doing things, Patrick would stop them in several different creative ways. Through Coaching he realized that not only didn't he trust in his employees that he hired, but that he didn't trust his own decisions to hire them in the first place!

He was double sabotaging himself! By **forcing his solutions, his** way of doing things, **he** created a **false reality** of a successful completion. In the short run he got things accomplished the way **he** thought was best, but in reality, he was setting himself up for failure by not creating strong leaders and employees who had confidence in their capabilities and could get the job done.

Can you imagine how huge this was when he finally got it! It wasn't easy. It took weeks of Coaching and taking an honest hard look at himself! We took his determined spirit and applied it where it could really make a difference – **in himself.** Determined to enjoy the fruits of his labor, not only financially but with peace of mind and a well balanced life, Patrick was open for Coaching, open to new ideas, open to looking at things from another perspective. Suddenly new possibilities opened up!

People around him were lit up, full of ideas and excitement as they now felt valuable to the organization. Patrick now had a new tool of his own! Through Coaching he learned to interrupt the old patterned behavior and move past that which once stopped him!

He created an atmosphere of success for himself and his employees! An atmosphere that fostered measurable results in financial and personal gain for everyone that worked for his company! With joy like this filling the atmosphere imagine what results could be possible for you and your business!

*Although the Coaching situation is real, the name has been changed to protect confidentiality.*

# Reprogramming Your Computer

Change your thinking, change your life! We've heard it a million times! Over and over again, whither through our Bible Studies, Church Services, secular authors and speakers, the message remains the same; *"our outer life is a direct result of our inner thinking"*. But what does that mean? How do go about creating results we want in a certain area, especially if we've been dealing with the same old issues? How do we start? How do we get rid of old behavior patterns that no longer serve us? How do we implement and maintain new *chosen* behavior patterns.

Let's take a closer look at one organization that got intentional about celebrating diversity and creating unity amongst their employees.

In order to effect change in the workplace we need more than just an occasional training session. The challenging news is that change happens slowly over a period of time. The good news is that it can happen with the proper tools in place. One of those tools is Coaching. Taking concepts and programs introduced at a training session into follow up group coaching sessions will ensure the success of your individual employee retention rate thus creating company success as a whole.

Using diversity training as our model today, we go deep into the thinking patterns of individuals and challenge their core beliefs. In taking a deeper look into how and why we believe certain things, we are then faced with *"Reframing our thoughts"* around that particular topic aka *"Reprogramming your computer/your mind"!* We come to recognize as human beings we are thinking, judging, and accessing machines that need to be reprogrammed daily!

Getting *"Intentional"* and *"Thinking on Purpose"*, are the keys to your success in this process. *"Noticing"* what we are thinking, interrupting those thoughts and replacing them with statements such as *"Up until now, I believed……..and "There must be another way of looking at this………."* are the continued Coaching tools used to reprogram that awesome computer – our minds! And as we continue to be open to this coaching process we become much better human beings relating to each other, thus creating an atmosphere of acceptance and cooperation increasing our productivity on the job as well as improved relationships!

I realize this might sound a bit simplistic and it actually is! Simple but not easy! Simple solutions to a very complex human mind that wants to judge and access every situation, every person and by the way be the one that shows up right every time! What will you choose today? Take on challenging yourself daily and watch your life take on new meaning. What was once exceptionally hared becomes much easier as you begin to put into action the principals that Christ came to teach us! As a man thinks, so he is! We must renew our minds daily!

- *Bolded italic word/statements are some of the tools used by Sinatra Solutions in Executive Coaching.*

## Karen's Story

## Noticing

Last months column included many tools that I use in my Coaching/Training Programs to assist individuals in identifying where they get stopped/stuck and how to move past those blockers. Today we are going to take a closer look at one of those key blockers and the tools that assist us in creating the success we desire!

During a corporate training surrounding the topic of "Celebrating Diversity", Karen began to see how she truly was a "judging assessing machine" and how that was costing her in relating to her co-workers. Using the noticing exercises helped her to see that she was constantly judging and assessing those around her. Although she felt she was pretty open when it came to inclusion, there were still those hidden places where she held some old prejudice thoughts concerning people who look/act different than herself. It was quite an eye opener for her.

As you being to "notice" your thoughts, you then have access to "reframing" them in the particular way you desire. You will begin to acquire the skill of you running your thoughts, rather than your thoughts running you! As human beings we just can't help it.

Watch for it yourself – as you are ready this article you are already sitting in judgment as to the concepts I am presenting! You are making your mind up about this concept and forming an opinion about me! Got ya! And that's ok. As long as you are in a human body living on the planet earth, you will be doing this. The good news is that as you begin to apply some of these tools you will have an easier and easier time managing yourself!

You will have the opportunity to see if what you are thinking really lines up with who you say you are in life or if there are some old, negative thoughts that keep trying to invade your mind/your computer; a virus if you will!!!

So just like a computer can catch a virus your mind can too. It's so important to live life aware – noticing your thoughts when you meet a new person, or come in contact with an old friend, hear a new concept, visit a new place, and meet others who look/act differently than yourself. What will you catch yourself thinking and how will you "reframe" that thought?

There is so much power in this simple exercise. Begin today and watch your life begin to change. Commit yourself today and watch how you too will begin to "Create Success Everywhere you go"!

*Although the Coaching situation is real, the name has been changed to protect confidentiality.*

## Mary's Story

## When is enough...enough?

The Word of God tells us to look at things not as they are but as we know they could be. To speak things into existence is the power we hold when the Holy Spirit is living inside of us. The power of life and death lye in our tongues! Our thoughts control our atmosphere; pull down every thought that is not of Him; focus on whatever is good, righteous and holy.

Believe everything/anything is possible when we are moving in the power of Pentecost! Speak to the mountain and tell it to move – Believe – Have Faith – Don't give up – Wait on Him – Stand on His Word - The Joy of the Lord is our Strength – Through Him all things are possible! But when is enough, enough?

Mary was determined to make her marriage work. Even though chronologically she was getting up there in age, she was a young believer. Ever since she came in contact with Jesus, she hungered for more and more understanding and wisdom in applying the Word of God in her life. Every Sunday service lit her up. Every Bible study gave her encouragement.

The more she studied the Word, the more she became convicted. Already an optimist, as she emerced herself in the Word, she became a prisoner of Hope! So what was the problem? Let's take a closer look.

Mary's focus was on changing herself, her husband and her children. She worked hard and long at identifying her strengths and weakness over the years and grabbed onto the tools that were available to try to "fix" herself. She not only took her inventory but did this with her husband and children! Something inside her kept driving her to point out the areas she believed needed to be "fixed" in those around her.

This drove her family crazy, and unknown to them, she was quite miserable inside as well! The constant judgment of herself and others drove her further and further away from the Peace she so desired. But she couldn't seem to stop. She couldn't seem to "give up" this behavior, this belief, until we took a closer look.

Behind that determined drive was a huge mass of fear. Fear was running her life and she couldn't see it because she was consumed with "fixing", "managing" everything! She took the principals based on the Word of God and did what she did best; tried to "fix" the problem by layering some Word over it! And as you can image, things only got worse! She became tired and weary and found herself inside of the question, when is enough, enough?

It's only when she become so frustrated, so exhausted of trying to be the director of the universe, so tired of being sick and tired, that she was then ready to try something different then what she was used to doing. Using the visualization of Jesus on the cross, together we brought all her problems/concerns and laid them down at Jesus' feet. Turning it (them) over to God, believing and trusting in His power to change situations and people was the hardest thing in the world for her to do.

It was easier to look for the answers outside of herself. Look for the answers in the "what if's", and the "only if they would", etc., etc. Looking outside of ourselves for the answers to problems is like taking a shower and expecting the water to go inside of us. The only way to get the water inside is to drink it!!!

Her focus had to change! Her focus had to be on turning over her life to God daily. Every morning she began on her knees using this visualization and asking/expecting God to handle her life problems along with the rest of the world! After all, isn't this what we're commissioned to do? She struggled with wanting to pick up the problems throughout the day and micro manage them.

Instead she would quietly ask God for His help. She'd pick up a reading, or take a deep breath, or close her eyes momentarily and see the vision of Jesus on the cross, anything she could do to not slip into old behavior patterns. It's not easy to change a behavior pattern, but it can be done! Looking inward at the fear base she was operating from, was the key here. It was inside of her that needed eternal optimism! Giving up the constant strain of judgment on herself and others and keeping her focus on herself was the only way to go! Enough was finally enough!

*Although the Coaching situation is real, Mary is the name used to protect confidentiality.*

# Jesus Story

## Everyone is Welcome – Part I

Seems to me that Jesus loved everyone; He had an endless reservoir of compassion and forgiveness. He didn't expect people to come up to his level; He ministered to them by going to where they were at. He approached them with love, understanding and an absence of judgment. Then why do we sit in judgment of everyone/everything everyday?

In most of my trainings, motivational speaking engagements and coaching conversations I introduce this distinction: "As human beings we are thinking, judging, assessing machines". Unconsciously we are assessing every situation we go in, every person we meet and we formulate a judgment. Right about now you might be thinking – no I don't! But let me point out that you are already judging and assessing as you are reading this article! Think about it!

As you are reading your mind is making up opinions and judgments with each and every sentence you read! Until you begin to notice that this is actually an everyday, every moment occurrence, it will continue onward with no awareness on your part as to the how and why's, your life keeps showing up as it is. Confused? Let's take a closer look.

Things happen to us throughout our development and unconsciously opinions and judgments are created. If we never take the time to listen to the "chatter" that goes on inside our minds, if we never take the responsibility for how we are thinking, and never challenge that thought process, we create our lives from the perspective of those limiting beliefs that we developed as we went through the many circumstances of our lives! Still confused? Let's look a bit closer.

Maybe you have a prejudice against another person because of how they look or how they act. Or maybe you have a belief that your way of worship is the only or the best way. Or maybe you feel that your race is better than someone else's. Maybe men are the stronger sex and women really shouldn't be in the pulpit. What ever you're thinking at this moment, as you read this - is just that! It's your thought!

It belongs to you. Your thinking it and you will create your world around you according to that perception! You can and will find every argument and every bible verse to support your thinking structure! The key here is going deep inside yourself, examining why and how you came to believe that particular judgment, bring it to God, and compare it to His Word by really studying the whole context verses just one fragment of a sentence.

Pray, pray and pray some more then utilize this tool: "There must be another way of looking at this". Challenge yourself, challenge your thought structure.

Everyone was welcomed in Jesus' presence. He met people where their at. He ministered to them through love. He was Love in expression. His presence invited those around Him to draw closer. He didn't care if you were male or female, black or white, rich or poor, fat or skinny, Christian or non believer. He didn't even care what denomination you were! Were there denominations back then? I think not. So why do we need to judge and assess who is right, who will go to heaven?!

There must be another way of looking at this. How about we leave the judging up to God, and use Jesus as our example and way shower and come together in the name of Love. Look for the similarities with your brother. Celebrate the differences with your sister. Come together in unity and begin to really create "Com unity"! Build bridges, create relationships and by your example you too will draw people closer to Christ!

*Dear friends, let us practice loving each other, for love comes from God and those who are loving and kind show that they are the children of God, and that they are getting to know him better. But if a person isn't loving and kind, it shows that he doesn't know God – for God is love. I John 4:7-8*

*Dear friends, since God loved us as much as that, we surely ought to love each other too. I John 4:11*

*"And so I am giving a new commandment to you now – love each other just a much as I love you. Your strong love for each other will prove to the world that you are my disciples." John 13:34-35*

*"Little children, let us stop just saying we love people; let us really love them, and show it by our actions". I John 3:18*

## Andrew's Story

## Everyone is Welcome – Part II

Andrew finally found Jesus! He knew that his church was the best! He found the key to the kingdom and he was determined to set everyone, anyone around him free! He plowed forward with his Bible bashing to anyone who came within 10 feet of him. Yes I said Bible bashing. He hit them left and right with the word of God and tried to win them through their guilt and condemnation. Unsuccessful in his attempts he couldn't see why they weren't listening! Surely they could see their evil ways as he pointed them out. Surely they could see how they need to repent and be saved! Why wouldn't they listen?!

As we took a closer look during our Coaching calls, Andrew began to see that his enthusiasm as a newly saved Christian was quite overwhelming to his family and friends that weren't saved. He began to realize that in his excitement he began using the little bit of Word he was beginning to learn and use it in a way that was turning others off! He meant well but his actions were not getting the results he desired. Because his heart was in the right place he was open to some Coaching around this situation.

We explored Andrew's past. We went back and took a look at all the times prior to him actually getting saved. There were many times people approached him and tried to get him to see the light! But often he would resist. He even had friends and family that refused to associate with him, the sinner, because he wouldn't listen to them!

The more we talked about those specific incidents the more Andrew got in touch with how he hated it when others thought they knew what was best for him. He realized that he might have come to Christ sooner if those around him were the example of the Love that Jesus was expressing rather than just hitting him with scripture after scripture. The words they used along with the attitude they were expressing wasn't exactly inviting.

Any of this sound familiar? Maybe you've been a victim of this kind of behavior and/or maybe you are a bit like Andrew. Only you can examine your life and decide if what you're doing is working for you and others. Only you can make a decision to change your behavior, your way of looking at things. When you take the time to examine your life in a way that is truly honest, you then have access to creating a new future filled with the possibility to create the results you desire!

Think about Jesus – think/study his behavior; how he approached people and situations. Think about the expression of love he was to anyone/everyone he came in contact with. I believe it is our commission to become as Christ like as we possibly can! We have the ultimate example of unconditional love in expression – Jesus! Don't just study to memorize the Word – Study to embody the Word! Put into action the Christ nature Jesus came to teach us!

Put on love, be love, express love, show love and continue to ask Jesus to help you on this walk. It isn't easy. No one said it was. Look how Jesus expressed Love; remember what he did for each and every one of us!

*"For God loved the world so much that he gave his only Son so that anyone who believes in him shall not perish but have eternal life." John 3:16*

*"May our Lord Jesus Christ himself and God our Father, who has loved us and given us everlasting comfort and hope which we don't deserve, comfort your hearts with all comfort, and help you in every good thing you say and do. 2 Thessalonians 2:16,17*

*"Since you have been chosen by God who has given you this new kind of life, and because of his deep love and concern for you, you should practice tenderhearted mercy and kindness to others. Don't worry about making a good impression on them but be ready to suffer quietly and patiently. Be gentle and ready to forgive; never hold grudges. Remember, the Lord forgave you, so you must forgive others. Colossians 3:12,13*

*\*Although the Coaching situation is real, the name used to protect confidentiality.*

**Conclusion:**

Although I have had tremendous success in impacting audiences from 10 – 500 as a Key Note Speaker, I realize it takes much practice to change a pattern/behavior, that's why I am a Coach! Through regular scheduled Coaching calls I have been privileged to assist so many individuals, companies, organizations in identifying and moving past the obstacles that stopped them dead in their tracks! Utilizing the amazing tools of my particular system of Coaching, together we have been able to realize both internally and externally tremendous success!

I don't have to say so, just visit my web site and read the hundreds of testimonies from real people with real names and contact info. My clients sell me! After their initial consultation, I point them to my web site and there they find all the evidence of "Measurable Results" that inspire them to get into action. My prayer for you today is that you found yourself in some of the examples I provided in this e-book, had a couple of ah – ha moments and will begin to apply some of the tools and techniques that have been proven to work.

Below for your review is what I call my "Creative Discovery Tool Box". Use it as a reminder when you get stuck. Don't be too hard on yourself! Remember as they say Rome wasn't built in a day! It took many years for you to develop your thinking, your ways, core beliefs, and habits and it's going to take some time and intentionality to move past them. Begin with one small step! Begin today and watch what God does! The choice is yours! What will you chose?

## Anna Marie Sinatra

INSPIRATIONAL ORIGIONAL QUOTES
Check out Sinatra Solutions on FaceBook...
...original pictures that go with many of the quotes!
www.facebook.com/SinatraCoach/

*Where there's a will, there's a way!*
*Anna Marie Sinatra*

*It doesn't matter where you come from - it matters where you end up!*
*Anna Marie Sinatra*

*Every time you avoid something, your world gets smaller and smaller. You must take risks!*
*Anna Marie Sinatra*

*You devalue someone when you don't look at them when they are speaking.*
*Anna Marie Sinatra*

*Why are you there? Don't you want to move on? The first step you must take is to make a decision.*
*Anna Marie Sinatra*

*What is it that keeps me from seeing myself as qualified as a professional when I'm in a group of professionals who are my colleagues?*
*Anna Marie Sinatra*

*If I judge myself harshly, I stay stuck. I will be gentle with myself as I take a honest, loving look, so I continue to stay open and willing for change.*
*Anna Marie Sinatra*

*Move from just surviving our lives every day, to living our lives on purpose with Joy.*
*Anna Marie Sinatra*

*My illusions keep me stuck. I must die to my illusions!*
*Anna Marie Sinatra*

*God responds only to love!*
*Anna Marie Sinatra*

Keep setting standards no matter how many times people have disappointed you. Life is all about your intention... Your integrity!!!
Anna Marie Sinatra

Notice your thoughts... You are empowered or dis-empowered according to your perceptions.
Anna Marie Sinatra

Are you a victim of your perceptions or are you victorious because of your perceptions?
Anna Marie Sinatra

The same principles that make a successful life, make a successful business.
Anna Marie Sinatra

A dream will only be a dream unless you are willing to take action. In order to have a successful life, job or business, you must plan ahead to develop it into reality.
Anna Marie Sinatra

Develop a clear vision and mission statement; then begin with one small step. The journey of a thousand miles begins with one small step!
Anna Marie Sinatra

Wake up 20 minutes earlier three times this week and plan three things you can do during the week to make your dream become reality.
Anna Marie Sinatra

Behind every complaint is a commitment.
Anna Marie Sinatra

Even if you don't have physical money in your hand... just keep working towards your goal. Don't stop short of the miracle!
Anna Marie Sinatra

The ultimate secret... you manifest what you judge...
Anna Marie Sinatra

The Path to Happiness is the Relinquishment of judgment...
Anna Marie Sinatra

*Every time you avoid something, your world gets smaller and smaller. You must take risks!*
*Anna Marie Sinatra*

*Take an Honest look... and ask yourself... why am I here? Do I really want to move on? The first step is to make a decision.*
*Anna Marie Sinatra*

*If you judge yourself harshly you stay stuck. Be gentle with yourself and stay open and willing for change.*
*Anna Marie Sinatra*

*Illusions keep us stuck. We must die to our illusions.*
*Anna Marie Sinatra*

*God responds only to love!*
*Anna Marie Sinatra*

*The Path to Happiness is the Relinquishment of judgment...*
*Anna Marie Sinatra*

Go where you're celebrated... not tolerated...
*Anna Marie Sinatra*

Sometimes you have to go where you're tolerated... before you get celebrated...
*Anna Marie Sinatra*

A good leader knows how to follow.
*Leadership series, 1 of 3*
*Anna Marie Sinatra*

Individual leaders know how to follow.
*Leadership series, 2 of 3*
*Anna Marie Sinatra*

You cannot be a leader unless you are a follower.
*Leadership series, 2 of 3*

*Anna Marie Sinatra*

Life may not be the party we hoped for...
...but while we are here we might as well dance!
*Anna Marie Sinatra*

ARE YOU COACHABLE?
*Anna Marie Sinatra*

ARE YOU OPEN TO NEW IDEAS?
*Anna Marie Sinatra*

NOTICE WHAT YOU'RE THINKING!
*Anna Marie Sinatra*

GET COMFORTABLE WITH BEING UNCOMFORTABLE
*Anna Marie Sinatra*

COMPARING IS A PIT FALL
*Anna Marie Sinatra*

AS SOON AS THOSE NEGATIVE THOUGHTS FLOAT IN - INVITE THEM TO FLOAT RIGHT BACK OUT!
*Anna Marie Sinatra*

WHAT YOU RESIST - PERSISTS
*Anna Marie Sinatra*

EVERYONE IS CREATIVE
*Anna Marie Sinatra*

YOUR PERCEPTION BELONGS TO ONLY YOU
*Anna Marie Sinatra*

Stop negative patterns by declaring... UP UNTIL NOW... then replace thought with positive affirmation!
*Anna Marie Sinatra*

TURN PROBLEMS INTO POSSIBILITIES
*Anna Marie Sinatra*

What you believe you can achieve
*Anna Marie Sinatra*

Living in the Flow…
*Anna Marie Sinatra*

Everywhere you go… there you are!
*Anna Marie Sinatra*

When given the opportunity… practice patience.
*Anna Marie Sinatra*

Information is powerful only when you act on it. Get into action today!
*Anna Marie Sinatra*

Envision the end result!
*Anna Marie Sinatra*

WIN ~ WIN… look for the similarities NOT the differences!
*Anna Marie Sinatra*

Communication ~ how am I listening?
*Anna Marie Sinatra*

Reacting vs. Responding
*Anna Marie Sinatra*

Expectations ~ set up for failure or necessary step?
*Anna Marie Sinatra*

F.E.A.R. ~ Fearlessly Easy After Review
*Anna Marie Sinatra*

Get comfortable with being Uncomfortable
*Anna Marie Sinatra*

Sometimes you have to get comfortable in order to make other uncomfortable.
*Anna Marie Sinatra*

Life isn't fair, but it's still good.
*Anna Marie Sinatra*

When in doubt, just take the next small step.
*Anna Marie Sinatra*

Life is too short to waste time hating anyone.
*Anna Marie Sinatra*

Don't take yourself so seriously. No one else does.
*Anna Marie Sinatra*

Pay off your credit cards every month.
*Anna Marie Sinatra*

Save for retirement starting with your first paycheck.
*Anna Marie Sinatra*

Up until now…
*Anna Marie Sinatra*

You don't have to win every argument. Agree to disagree.
*Anna Marie Sinatra*

Cry with someone. It's more healing than crying alone.
*Anna Marie Sinatra*

When it comes to chocolate, resistance is futile.
*Anna Marie Sinatra*

No one falls in love by choice, it is by CHANCE.
*Love series, 1 of 3*
*Anna Marie Sinatra*

No one stays in love by chance, it is by WORK.
*Love series, 2 of 3*
*Anna Marie Sinatra*

And no one falls out of love by chance, it is by CHOICE.
*Love series, 3 of 3*
*Anna Marie Sinatra*

It's OK to get angry with God. He can take it.
*Anna Marie Sinatra*

65484163R00029

Made in the USA
Middletown, DE
27 February 2018